HOUND

by Leya Roberts
illustrations by Rick Geary

Harcourt Brace & Company

Orlando Atlanta Austin Boston San Francisco Chicago Dallas New York Toronto London

Miss Dowd found a nice hound at the town pound. The hound was brown, with long jowls and a loud howl. Miss Dowd called her hound Scout.

2

Scout liked to dig in the
ground. He dug up big round
mounds in Miss Dowd's yard.
Miss Dowd frowned and
scowled. "No, Scout!"

In the house, Scout lounged about and bounded around. He pounced on Miss Dowd's couch, leaving brown hair all over it. Miss Dowd frowned and scowled. "Down, Scout!"

At night, Scout howled. What a loud sound! He jumped over the fence and prowled around the town, growling at cats. Again Miss Dowd frowned and scowled. "No, Scout!"

People in the town frowned and scowled at Miss Dowd.

"Scout howls!" shouted a crowd. "Scout jumps over our fences! Scout growls at our cats!"

Miss Dowd slouched on her couch. "You're a nice hound, Scout. But you have to go back to the pound."

7

Miss Dowd took Scout back to the pound. Scout crouched down and pouted.

"Now, now, don't pout," said Miss Dowd. Scout howled and howled as Miss Dowd drove away. What a sad sound!

9

Miss Dowd sat on her couch, frowning and scowling. After an hour, Miss Dowd shouted, "I miss Scout!"

Miss Dowd went back to the pound. "Come out, Scout! I have a plan." Scout wagged his brown tail and howled a loud, happy howl.

Later Miss Dowd drove south out of town. "Jump out now, Scout," said Miss Dowd, "and see our new house. This is our farm!"

Scout bounded around,
howling and yowling. Scout dug
up the ground. Miss Dowd
didn't frown or scowl. Miss
Dowd planted seeds. Scout was
a good plow hound!

At night, Scout prowled around and howled. Miss Dowd didn't frown or shout. The cows and chickens were safe with Scout around.

14

"I'm proud of you, Scout,"
cried Miss Dowd. "Now I know—
you're a farm hound, not a
town hound. Now come in the
house."

"It's a couch for you!" said
Miss Dowd proudly. Scout
jumped onto the couch and
howled. "You're a nice hound,
Scout," said Miss Dowd.